I Aspire to Inspire

Kristina Darby

KRISTINA DARBY

DEDICATION

Ok so BOOM!! My moms, HalfPint, this one is for you sis. I hope one day our growth is together, nonetheless I am thankful for you and all you have taught me. My homies til the end whom I still owe coins, Bettina and I would never forget you Eva. You two women saw me through hard times and held my tears when I could not dam them myself. Shakevia BoomQuisha Richards, sis thanks for seeing the leader in me and forcing me to seek the knowledge in depth because your ass needed to know with bottomless questions. Jermarsha and Nadia....at a level of life where self was unknown I appreciate the mirrors you two forced in my face. Ashley....my SisterFriendCousinEarOfTheYear... you told my mom in the backyard of our duplex on Cromwell, "your daughter can preach, and she gone change lives one day", when we were children. I do not know if you remember or not but sis, it's been you all the time. My fucking NaNa.....she always was my spiritual guide. My G, Mrs. Coleman to the hood, Ida Mae to her peers, A FUCKING SHERO to me. My Tootsie, Shyneica you made me strong in ways I did not know I could be strong in. Last but definitely first in my life, MY POODIE!!!!!!! My little brother is my reason for it all. I can't tell you what you are capable of being if I ain't showing you the possibilities.

For the longest time I had the question, "WHY?", about everything from food to politics to life to psyche to the system, you
name it. I used to be pissed because my why was mostly si-
lenced, rarely answered. So when I was old enough I started
searching for it myself. I no longer depended on others for the
answer. Repeat this aloud daily, "TRUTH IS EXPOSED BY EXPERI-
ENCE!" It took time to get to this revelation, but I can guide you
to it faster and easier. So thankful I can alter or halt others from
going through what I went through.

Ever felt unworthy? Unloved? Unlearned? Emptiness? Unheard?
Desired death? I have felt all of these things combined, separate-
ly, and often. It took me learning to love myself, value myself,
respect myself, and defining myself for me. Self work takes
time, and it takes dedication. It takes accountability. It takes
determination, but most importantly the desire to grow has to
be there. Nothing in our lives happen without us choosing it. We
choose the karma we receive by the way we treat others and
ourselves. No matter how small the doing it brings conse-
quences, you choose whether it be good or bad.

A lot of us mask our true self with coping mechanisms from
trauma we have yet to heal from. We do not realize the one that
suffers the most from our doings is ourself. We do not want to
hold parents accountable. You can't fix a problem without fixing
the roots first.

CONTENTS

I Aspire to Inspire

ACKNOWLEDGMENTS

Yooooooo....you fuck with me huh? You bought my book or took the time to read it, even if it's just this page. I'm thankful and forever indebted to you. Thank you so much. So when I first started writing this it was taking forever. I was writing for other people tho. I had no reason or goal to write, plus I thought books had to have a certain look to be considered a book. I sit here at the Big Blue Back-Packers in Cape Town, South Africa writing this here tho. This book is for all my snap chat followers that has been asking for it for years. This book is for my followers on Instagram asking for tangibles. You see nothing in life is normal. I learned that long back. No two humans have the same story. You and another could be born to the same parents, attend the same schools, choose the same job, attend the same college, get the same career AND STILL ya both will tell a different story. So buckle up and enjoy.

I Aspire to Inspire

You First, or Them Not At All

Imagine settling to make someone else happy and they leave you for someone who makes them happy. They put themselves first and you are mad they did not settle with you, instead of thanking them and seeing the good in goodbye. The lesson at hand is to put you first. Regardless of how you think it will make others feel, always choose you and your happiness. Start putting yourself first. Do what makes you happy. If you are easily enticed by others or think you need to cheat to supplement your happiness, you're settling. Pretty sure there are other things and red flags, you ignore, that bother you. You don't have to wait until others express their discomfort to express yours. You don't have to go tic for tac when an issue arise if you communicating for understanding. You can get your point across without bringing up an old issue to one up their issue with you. You can hear them out and thoroughly communicate your issue then ask for an amnesty hour to clear all issues and then bring it up. FIRST CLEAR THEIR ISSUE!!!

My Own Rules

No two relations are the same. Create your own rules. What works for you? What are you wanting your best friend/life partner to be? You can't look at someone else ship and call it goals. You don't know how many oceans it crossed during storm season. How many repairs it has had to look that immaculate. You don't know how many miles on that motor. Who knows the behind the scene of that photo op? You never really know what kind of darkness people are hiding behind their "world" facade. So many of us care what others think of us so we show them what they'd give us good feedback on. Imagine a world of truth walkers, talkers, and seekers. Your relationship will never be perfect, but you can decide more happy days than not. You can choose a mate that actually loves their self so you will know they really love you. Their looks won't keep you happy nor raise your seeds. A healthy mental state and personality is more important than a good looking one.

GOODbye

Find the good in goodbye. New beginnings await you. A healthier love. A more radiant authentic smile. Some people don't think you will ever cut them off so they will be as toxic as you tolerate. Toxic people have no boundaries, thats why they push/test yours. If a person make you feel like shit why continue allowing them? They're a distraction, a karmic relation. A person that is for you, would not hurt you intentionally; and when unintentional they're apologetic and fix it. You can't receive the love you need holding on to the love you think you want. If you find yourself intentionally hurting someone, "SPOT CHECK!!", check yourself on the spot. Hold yourself accountable. Apologize to them and to yourself. Apologize to yourself because you are your words. Fix the behavior as well. Check yourself every time you find yourself being spiteful. Nothing good comes of it. Karma has no expiration date. Say goodbye to negative behaviors, negative humans, negative thoughts of yourself, toxic humans, toxic environments, toxic habits AND ACTUALLY MEAN IT!!!!

Communication

(or lack thereof)

Communication is a huge problem for most. Some reasons more obvious than others. A lot of us had our voices muted as children, whether we like to admit it or not. Being able to thoroughly communicate is necessary for any relationship to succeed. When you're raised in a toxic environment where communication is lacking you become a lacking ass adult. You lack the social skills to thoroughly communicate and have your voice heard without feeling small or being defensive. You lack the ability to communicate when you feel disrespected or used, out of fear you will create an enemy or anger the person. You lack the ability to stand up for yourself. Prioritize using your voice. If you're not letting others know how, what, and why you feel the way you do, you allow them to fill in the blanks. You allow them to treat you how they please and not how you choose or desire. When you mute your own voice you tend to want others to be quiet when they use their voice in ways you're uncomfortable with. If you lack growth you'll notice if you observe yourself; your circle won't/don't change, your hobbies the same as a few years ago, your happiness is based on things external, your life is a hamster wheel (whether you admit it or not), this is just a few obvious signs. When we were younger, most of us, didn't have much of a say in our own lives. So we mastered going with the flow to please others

and not self. Thats a coping mechanism. Remember most of
your life lessons were learned during your innocent stage
when you couldn't decipher right from wrong, left from right,
toxic or healthy. You're grown now beloved. You can say who,
what, when, where, how long, and be heard. You can choose.
You can decide. You're the only constant in your life, permanent one that is. Appreciate yourself and communicate with
yourself. You are your own lifeline to the world now. You're
the sole custodian of your life.

Self!

In order to achieve all the things you wish for in others you must BE THESE THINGS FOR SELF!! You can't ask someone to love you if you don't know how to love yourself or know your own love language. In order to love you have to know what kind you want. You have to know what kind you desire. If you don't know the kind you desire you'll accept anything and settle, or you'll go through the cycle of settling until you find one that feels like home. You'll break yourself more than help yourself by doing the latter. Fall in love with yourself and you'll know when the right one is for you. Don't settle whatsoever. The minute it seems off and you realize it's not for you let it go. You don't need three strikes. You don't need to collect any closure. Just communicate and walk. Do not compromise your peace for anyone. Be definite they're for you before giving them all the parts of you that were once broken. To be definite you must be willing to grow. Growth is unconventional and very uncomfortable. In comfort lies stagnancy, self doubt, lack of learning, settlement, grief, misery, depression, stress, suicidal thoughts, missing knowledge, and acceptance of less than your worth. You can't give any part of you to others that you don't know. Life is funny. If you're questionable enough it comes full circle showing you who you used to be in other people; this is only to show you exactly why you're going through what you are on that level with that specific karmic relation. At one point you were giving all the karma you're receiving. To live a life in abundance you must give a life of abundance. Karma has no expiration, only an owner. What exactly are you requesting of your higher self with your current actions?

Free Your Spirit

Learn to express your feelings freely. Don't hide your emotions nor fear how they will make others feel. Those that mind don't matter and those that matter don't mind. Communicate your feelings as best you can in words. If the issue angers you request a break or amnesty moment to say it exactly the way you're feeling it. Do not intentionally hurt others just because or due to you feeling they hurt you. If you didn't mean it that way why not apologize for making them feel a way when it wasn't your intentions? Being apologetic does not make you weak, it means you care. You care how you make others feel. You know the power of words and the lasting effect they have. Caring about others will create a bubble of people that also care about you.

Stress

STRESS?! Whats that? ITS YOU OVERTHINKING!!! Stress is literally you overthinking. Whether you stress out or be calm the outcome remains uncontrollable. You can do your best and prepare for the worst without stressing. When you feel stressed, STOP!! Whatever you're doing should come to a complete halt. Think about the last time you felt this way.....what was the outcome? Your stress changed anythings besides the rate of your heartbeat? Seek solutions with the mentality, "regardless of what happens, if I do not die this was a test, a lesson, and a blessing." You need your bad experiences as much as your great. Appreciation goes further. Life flows freely. You can't control the karma but you can control your reaction to it. See everything as educational and not problematic, and watch how your life change. If you don't learn the lesson it will be repeated. It is repeated because the lesson didn't change you, you got angry and stayed the same. Change comes from within. The lessons are from your higher self.

Choose You

So many of us count on things outside of self to maintain. We slave ourselves day in and day out physically, mentally, emotionally, and/or financially, then we put self last on the thank you list. No one but you could have gotten that done. If you had not desired to get it done, you would not have. If you didn't work hard for that degree you wouldn't have graduated. If you didn't desire change you'd stay the same. Karma is a full circle. All that you do, be it good or bad, is coming back to you. Nothing happens to you by mistake. You created this. You would change your environment if you were being compensated to do so, so why not do it for a healthy mental state? Once you've tried something and realize it does not work for you, LET IT GO ASAPTUALLY!! We hurt ourselves by holding on longer than we should. Pain comes to teach us lessons. If it is hurting you more than it's helping you, thats a clear indicator IT IS NOT FOR YOU! Toxicity only thrives where it is fed. Stop enabling the behavior. They will either change because they love you, or be selfish and stay the same which means they don't deserve you!

Celebration or Funeral
(Who's to say)

Death is our only common denominator, yet so many of us live in fear of it. It is coming whether you live making others happy, or if you live for you. Its coming whether you get that raise, open that business, or slave for someone else. Just because you put things on hold doesn't warrant you'll be here to get it done, so whats the hold up? Bet on yourself every time. Believe you deserve what your heart desire and don't settle until you receive it. Stop waiting for others to see your worth. Value yourself. I always wondered why we celebrate birth yet mourn death. We live everyday as if tomorrow is promised and when we lose someone we took for granted we stress ourselves in their afterlife instead of celebrating who they were and what they meant to us. Death is inevitable and time will not stop for your procrastination. DO IT DO IT NOW!!

Or Was It.......

Last time was the last time! We repeat lessons with people. If you notice your new mates behavior reminding you of your last mate R U N!!!!!!! You don't have to wait thirty days to get the picture. We get the very things we don't want until we fine tune our tolerance for what we DO WANT! You can't get who you desire until you know what it is specifically. You'll receive something that looks identical but its fraternal, under no circumstances do you settle. I said I wanted a man who was willing to grow, but I didn't say grow in real time together so I kept getting men that would say,"I'm a work in progress." They weren't progressing at all. We'd discuss the issue today and six days later they'd be back doing it. They'd excuse their behavior with, "people don't change overnight." I wasn't asking for perfection just accountability. Why make excuses if you're growing and get a reminder you're relapsing? People can actually grow overnight if they care enough about the person asking. If you tell me you don't like cherries I'll never buy you anything cherry again. I am trying to learn you and be your equal complement.

You want me to call instead of texting then I'm calling for communication unless you initiate a text conversation or it's something small. I respect boundaries as I expect the same. Reciprocity is everything in this world. Don't allow people to do things to you that you know you'd never do to them. Get specific with your boundaries and human garden qualifications. Your tribe will get real familiar, spiritually. Stand firm in and on who and what you are.

FEAR

Fear? What the fuck is that, even? Why are you afraid? Do you not trust yourself? What is there to fear with your strength? Do you not know who got you through the last time you thought would take you out? Do you not know the voice in your head? You can get through this and everything else as long as you desire so. You first have to believe in Y O U!! Step out on you. You can't climb a staircase by simply standing and staring at the stairs. You have to take the first step to get to the second one and every step after that one. You'll never see the penthouse view if your focus is on the buildings lobby because of a rude receptionist the first day. Don't allow others behavior to dictate yours. I don't care how mad you are I can read you and go back to my happiness when it comes to my peace and growth. Just because your routine is what you've always done doesn't mean you can't find a new route tomorrow. If you live your life fearing what if, you're going to wake up dead one day wondering, "what if I had just lived?" Focus on the lesson. Whether the outcome is good or bad it was something you needed to go through to grow. The unknown could be your next big break, and you have the audacity to not get it because of fear? Oh ok

Self Check

Most of our growth is forced from an early if we are not taught bad things are lessons and needed as much as the good in your life. If it didn't get cold you would take the warm days as guarantees. So many of us have forgotten that death is inevitable so we take life for granted. If you notice your human garden, family, get a plucking every now and then. When it happens all of a sudden everyone loves one another and feed each other lies on how we will hang more. You blindly forget the issues that kept you from speaking on the regular in the first place. It doesn't stay that way long. If we learned to properly communicate, be it comfortable or uncomfortable, there'd be no problems. When communicating for understanding problems can't coexist, only be resolved. Learn to face every issue with understanding as the goal, otherwise whats the point? Stop holding on to people for the sake of titles. You're enabling their toxic behavior. If you just complain

with idle threats, you're teaching them how to treat you. You're basically saying, "Its ok to fuck me over as long as you listen when I bitch about it. You don'y have to hear me or fix the issue." If you allow people to hurt you over

and over again you're the problem not them. They're aware of their behavior. If and when you stop enabling it they'll eventually grow through it or find new enablers until growth is forced or they finally face their music and self heal.

Growth

A lot of people reach a level of comfortability and stop growing. You can see it in their actions and hear it in their words. They will question your growth and try to hinder it if you allow it. They will say slick shit like, "you think you're too much", "you're too sensitive", "you've changed". Be mindful and vocal about your feelings and emotions. Just because others are afraid to speak up doesn't mean you have to stay mute. Your speaking up and growth in real time can inspire someone else to grow.

The more you learn the more you realize just how stagnant you were because of F E A R(a taught behavior or is it)!! You can't grow from a comfort zone. As humans we are conditioned to be uncomfortable if forced or gratification is due. Growth gives the unseen. You don't receive materials or worldly possessions for it. Only spiritual level ups and understanding of self. You'll free yourself of toxicity and gain a healthy mental state and environment. Our problem as humans is we care more about our external, what others see, than our internal, how we feel. We are conditioned to care more about others thoughts of us more than our own revelations of self. Majority of our thoughts of self are placed there subconsciously by others outside of self in the form of a joke or "criticism". When you aren't taught to know you and trust you FIRST, thats the outcome. When you're unknowing of self its easy to look outside of self for all things self, be it love, affection, patience, guidance, a savior, hope, faith, amongst other things.

Forced Growth

Oftentimes our higher self will force growth, and we don't willingly grow on our own time. The issue with forced growth is you spend your time angry it happened instead of focusing on the lesson at hand being taught. We are angry at the circumstances, the outcome, the pain, ourselves, the world; instead of stepping back and removing ourselves from the situation and seeing the lesson for what it is. We respond from our level of understanding so the next level is foreign. Take note of your uncomfortable times, those are growing pangs. Not all losses are a lost. Some are greatness disguised as pain. Enablers, addictions, materials (you've acquired it once you can get it again), and so many other things are forced ejections. We miss a car note a few too many times, but each time you missed it you had the money you just spent it elsewhere. Thats your hand being forced. You don't need materials that you cherish over living. You live in this big house and can't afford the note going to bed miserable every night, but you refuse to let it go because you care what others think of you. The next level of you will force you out of your comfort zone. It's up to your current level of self dedication to becoming your best self on how the forced growth is conceived (accepted). Others thoughts won't manifest a better you because they've never been on the path you're headed so ignore their words about you, GOOD AND BAD ALIKE. Your past is your growth chart. How much have you learned? How much have you endured? How much of your growth was forced? To measure forced growth think back on all your heart breaks, loss jobs, missed connections because you were in your own way. Self healing is a lot of accountability for your part played in the you, you are becoming.

Karmic Relations

Have you ever heard of karmic love? I was never taught about it, and I wish I was, so some of my heart breaks would've been a bit easier to bear. Karmic love comes to teach you a lesson and it repeats itself in different people until you learn the lesson. It tears you down, makes you lie awake at night, sometimes causes tears, it's addictive, and a number of other things. I always thought there was a problem with me because I am damn near thirty and have yet to have a healthy relationship. There wasn't a problem at all. I just have lessons to learn and I am growing through them.

Remember when you first met a certain person, got a certain job, or attained a certain material possession? Remember how you based your happiness on material shit then as it disintegrated, the thing acquired got old? That's because happiness should come from within. It is a choice. You choose if you want to be angry, happy, sad, or whatever emotion you choose. Your reactions are all from you. Be it consciously decided or a robot decision, no one chooses it for you but you.

People will hurt you. Things will be lost. Career choices will change, but you my dear will forever be YOU!!!! So choose you every chance you get. Choose you over half love! Choose you over a job that doesn't care if you died today or tomorrow, because as soon as they hear of your death they start seeking someone to fill your shoes. I oftentimes hear my friends say,

"They lucky I need this job!", uhh sis that job needs you. See without you that position would be empty and they'd lose profit. If you are as good as you say you are at your talent why not get with your "friends" and pool your funds together to economically as a group start your own businesses. We are all born with a natural talent we can't escape. A lot of us lost that talent because of childhood trauma. Like if you were fit to be a barber. When you were younger you may have received countless ass beatings for cutting your hair so now you are reluctant unconsciously. You shy away from it but clippers call your name and haunt your dreams. Sweetie that's not a "weird" dream. That's your higher self trying to push you to be yourself. You work a desk job and you're miserable more than likely. Anything that's meant for you in life wouldn't bring you pain and misery, ON PURPOSE!!! Be it a job, a friend, a mate, a family member. We live in a world where everyone cares what others think of them but not everyone satisfies their own thoughts of themselves. Lemme break that down, DAWG NO ONE HAS TO SLEEP WITH YOUR THOUGHTS AT NIGHT BUT YOU!!!! If there are any thoughts that concern you, they should be tour own! It's a waste of life to go to sleep nightly miserable because you were busy pleasing the rest of the world and forgot about yourself along the way. No one has ever told us to get to know ourselves as a term of endearment. Its always "get a job", or "find a good man", or "keep your grades up to get in that college". Like what about getting to know myself so I can know if I even like working for someone else, or if I even like fucking men, or do I like critical thinking and self taught lessons instead of robot institutions that teach us all to be the same? So many of us live our lives for others and don't even know it. You buy designer clothes you don't even like to impress people you hardly know, then you are broke, financially, because you are living above your means to prove a point, no one except you knew you were proving!!! This is how they keep us in poverty. You think your brother's and sisters are your enemy. Instead of embracing one another in love and asking, "how's your spirit?", we greet one another with a frown or an angry stare. I smile at every black person I see regardless if they frown back or not. I often find myself asking them, "uhm you know me? I fuck ya man? Why you scolding me sis? I'm your ally." The mental issues are so deeply rooted because we've swept the pile over them CENTURY AFTER DECADE AFTER YEARS!!! We have been conditioned to mask our problems and wear a facade even if the facade is killing you.

Childhood Trauma

Ever find yourself having problems and you can't identify why are you having them, but you do know they exist? Let's discuss childhood trauma and its many effects. The first one is communication. You know how hard it is to communicate in a black household? I don't know who told black parents treating their children like slaves and not little humans was ok. You cannot CANNOT!!!!!! teach your child by speaking one lesson but living another. Children are visual sponges. If you smoke and drink in front of them and seem giddy and happy after, then they in turn will try it because you did. When your boss at work tells you, "don't be late" but he is always late what do you do? Your ass go ahead and start being later and later until its noticed. Why, because we are all visual learners and feel if you are doing it then why can't I? You can't tell your child, "you fight back everybody that raises a hand at you!", then turn around and beat your fucking child and expect them not to fight back. Thats contradicting. So fight the people in the street that disrespects me BUT if it's momma, daddy, or auntie let it fly? Thats that slave syndrome. Thats how masters kept their slaves in line. "You do as I say and not as I do" mentality. I think we get so wrapped up in being an adult we forget WE WERE ONCE CHILDREN. Now I can't tell you how to raise a child because I have yet to have one BUT I CAN TELL YOU what it feels like to be a child because I was once *one, and I* consider myself an adult child. I grew up to be childish. (Adulting was too hard and a bit too serious for the life I desire. I don't like wearing facades. I don't like doing things for the sake of doing them. I don't live to impress others. I don't care to have a million friends. I just desire the ability to be happy and live in my truth while allowing others the same space and mental capacity to do the same.) I am pretty sure, like me, most of you went through some shit as a child and said, "bruh I will never do this to my child!!" but look at you DOING THAT SHIT TO YOUR CHILD! Ever tried to communicate with your mom as a teenager? She was dismissive and Gawd forbid you decided you was gonna defend yourself against her, LMAO!!!! This is normal, yet toxic, in countless black households. When you can't communicate with your first responder it makes it hard to communicate with anyone in life. If your first responder loves you with conditions, you will think it's normal and accept half love from anyone who shows the slightest attention to you. Sometimes we don't even notice what we are doing because it's rare for someone to come into the black community and educate us on things like self love, self awareness, self discipline, knowing yourself, and dammit everything YOU! You can't benefit the world if you not healthy yourself. When we mention healthy these days everyone thinks physical. When I MENTION HEALTH I AM SPEAKING OF YOUR MENTAL AND SPIRITUAL HEALTH. When you know what toxic looks and feel like you want that for no one.

Let's page break so I can tell you my experience with childhood trauma

When I was younger I was adopted early on because my mom had me at fifteen but what she forgot was she was my aunt's live in babysitter. She got me back for all the wrong reasons. My mom took my adopted mom to court to get me back because (PRIDE) my adopted mom's sister called and told her, "you can't see your child unless my sister lets you!". So my mom flexed in black and white (on paper) and I spent my ninth year of life in a courtroom day in and day out. No one ever asked what I wanted or how it made me feel. I don't fault my mom for any of the things I went through, I fault her for not taking accountability when I told her how it made me feel. For many years I forced a relationship with my mother, regardless of how toxic it got, because I didn't have a dad and I felt I needed at least one parental to stay afloat. Little did I know I was postponing my healing and adding unnecessary toxicity in the name of I GOT MY MOMMA IN MY LIFE THO!! My mom is a great person don't get me wrong, she's just not the motherly type. The draw for me was when I was going through hell and she kicked me out her house then asked me to turn around and do favors for her like she wasn't shitting on me and telling me it was raining mud. What hurts me most with her is I told her how she hurt me and how toxic she was and instead of listening to understand she listened to respond and continues to do the same toxic shit with my little brother. When family members call to tell me I should talk to her I often ask them if they talked to her because she knows I said, "SEEK THERAPY BEFORE TRYING TO COME BACK IN MY LIFE!!". I was often the mom in our mother daughter relationship. I would call to talk about my problems and she would flip it to discuss her marital issues. I used to shower my mom with gifts because she chased men and money was love to her. I wanted to let her know I love you unconditionally regardless of what you do or say to me. When I was younger she always put her job over me, but she would get fired for her own personal bullshit. She'd say "I would get fired if I come to that award ceremony!!" but then end up fired anyways for about to fight someone. Sis, I would rather get fired for attending my child's award ceremony than ALMOST blows. You can't get back memories, but you can replace money day in and day out with any hustle known to man. Every important moment I ever had if it inconvenienced her she couldn't be there. You see, unconditional love isn't convenient. It's, "I'm doing this because I love you!". I have always just wanted someone to choose me. At the end of the day when the dusk settles THEY CHOOSE ME! I have yet to experience that. Every man I've dated to this date was a karmic relationship to teach me BITCH YOU GOTTA CHOOSE YOU FIRST THEN SOMEONE ELSE WILL TOO!!!! I guarantee you I got the message loud and clear this time y'all.

end page break

So childhood trauma comes in many shapes and forms. Communication is a huge problem in most childhood traumatic experiences. Most of us act our anger instead of speaking it for these reasons. We don't know how to fluently communicate our feelings without fear of hurting others or hurting ourselves most importantly. The next time you feel yourself getting angry, STOP! and breathe. Observe yourself and how you got to this point. Try to understand the triggers and the people you're around most when you feel this emotion. You control your emotions. When you allow others to control your emotions you become angry, happy, sad, elated, all at the pull of their string. When you get to know yourself you'll never give the power of your emotions to another unless they deserve it. Self worth goes hand in hand with knowing yourself and loving yourself.

I Mean

You can be everything a person needs, wants, values, and possess BUT if the person isn't appreciative, ready, or willing to reciprocate what are you even doing? Humans, or anything outside of self, is not your possession contrary to popular belief (Master this and you'll master human responses). We tend to strive to please others unaware of whose pleasing us. You can't pour from an empty cup. You can't give all of you if there's no replenish in sight. Whose gonna save you if you're saving the world? Be selfish with your peace yet selfless with your service to the world. Change your environment if your love isn't being reciprocated. You don't have to put up with disrespect or being hurt just to have a mate. Their replacement can't show up if the position occupied. Choose healthy relations over toxicity for the sake of saving face. State your intentions from the beginning unless you have something to lose.

What You Worth?

Ever get so accustomed to being treated a certain way that when someone else mentions it you get defensive; unbeknownst to you, you deserve better beloved. Our worth of self is shown to others by how we allow them to treat us. We should all value ourselves over things outside of us. You can't live without you. You CAN and HAVE lived without outside things and beings. People only do to you what you allow. What you feed will grow. If you keep going back after the first time it is no longer a mistake. They're now choosing to hurt you. You allowing it so why would they stop and/ or care? You're telling them with your actions you don't care regardless of what your words are. People that have yet to get to know self can easily fuck over the next with no remorse but, if it happens to them the world has ended. You treat people how you feel about yourself. Self love isn't taught. You have to desire it. You don't settle when you fully love yourself. You don't tolerate when you fully love yourself. Stop making the same choices because of fear. If you know this doesn't feel right, LEAVE IT!!

Who Are You?

Remember you are not others words, and they are not yours. What you eat don't make them shit and vice versa. If someone can anger you with their words, question your own thoughts on the topic. When you speak negative about yourself to yourself, aloud and subconsciously, you become those thoughts. When someone else mentions them you find truth in it because you say it to yourself. STOP THAT SELF DESTRUCTING SHIT!!! We often use materials to make up for our inadequate emotional behavior. Regardless of how you feel always speak positive to yourself. The world and things out of your control got the negatives covered for you. Speak and think positively. There's a lesson in everything. That in itself is the positive. You've the opportunity to learn. Learning is growing. Growth is always good. Love yourself completely. Include your flaws and your blind spots. You're human.

****Self Revelation****
(My truth)

When you've never felt worthy of love and someone shows you the slightest resemblance of the conditional love you're used to , you'll cling to it. Whether they value you, know your worth, treat you like shit, or not you'll be there as long as that fickle of love flames every now and then. It's a drug. It's a high. A narcissistic person feeds off of it. They prey on the weak. It gives them power and boost their ego. Ok ok ok I know I said my truth so let's get to it. Today while dancing and basking in the sunrise I was listening to Kelly Clarkson, "The Trouble With Love" and it dawned on me. We show off our love because we don't receive it as often as we should, well thats true in my case. I've always had conditional love, to be fair I think it's the only kind I know how to give in person. So when someone shows me love I show it off trying to prove to myself, "LOOK!, I'm worthy of love." That was the younger me. During my self healing, I'm ok with just my self love. I worked so hard on and for it. I taught myself and it was my most joyful ache to date. Showing off the love is a coping mechanism. You want others to think your life is perfect because you care what they think of you. I never wanted others to hurt or judge my mom so I acted as if she was the best mom in the world. I fucked up. When you don't hold others accountable you enable their behavior. They think they're doing amazing. Those that aren't knowing of self, including the old me, will blame anything outside of self to not be accountable or hold others accountable. You are what you allow. You are your environment. So I would praise my mom to others. I ignored her toxicity. I only spoke of it in secrecy. I praised ex boyfriends who were shitty to me. Knowing and loving self changes a lot in your life. You know shit and move differently. I stopped caring what others thought, only then did I begin to find true happiness. I went through a miscarriage. The guy I was with didn't know himself and neither did I at the time. So when I first loss the baby his main concern was me not telling anyone. He wanted to try and make another one instead. It was horrible for me. I'd already had miscarriages so I was really torn up. I was broken. How could this be? So I figured it was best to save face and go along with his plan. I, in no way, blame him for anything because I cared what people thought of me so I made the choice to ok his idea. So we tried and in my mind we'd got pregnant again but not in my body. I wanted it so bad that when a friend held a truth mirror to my face I cut her off. She'd done nothing wrong, but I wasn't ready to face my truths. I was in South Africa shortly after sitting in my apartment, I had rented through a rental app, I found a book, Knowing Yourself by Barry Long, that changed my life forever. That book had me talking my life over and holding myself accountable late nights turned early mornings with just myself. I read that book four times before I spoke to another human. (Lasted about four days.) I was already working on my healing but that turned my accountability leaf. It made me realize I was responsible for all my decisions. No one can choose for you but you.

Balance

Love is a balance. Relationships are a balance. You have to be as mature as humanly possible when involving someone else's feelings. You can't go around hurting people because you are hurting, and expect your heart to heal. You have to start walking in love, not fear. Stop fearing the unknown and brace yourself for it instead. Weigh your outcomes and prepare yourself as best you know how for them all to happen. You are going to experience it whether you live in fear or live in love. When you are living in fear you are easily provoked and or angered, you hurt people back that hurt you and play the blame game as an excuse for your actions. You love the pieces of you that you think others love. Love all of you. You can't be nor will you ever be perfect, you are gonna have flaws. Love yourself anyway. Accept the flaw and account for it. OWN IT! Catch yourself when it happens. Do not chastise yourself harshly. Treat yourself how you would treat your baby. Communicate with yourself about it. Do not spend too much time on it. After you go over the who, how, what, when, where of the situation LET IT GO! You deserve room to grow.

Tolerance

You become what you tolerate, subconsciously. What you allow will continue. You cannot live a life of happiness if your tolerance is high. You live a masked life. You tend to go along with shit to keep the peace, but peace for who, for what? If your peace was important to others you wouldn't be in a compromising position. Speak your truth. State your boundaries clearly. You don't have to tolerate toxicity for the sake of "possessing" a human. You can find another them or allow them to grow on their time not, so you're not hurt beyond repair in the process. The love of self and the tolerant self cannot coexist. Your subconscious will tell the truth whether you want it to or not.

Accountability

If you do not learn to hold yourself accountable, you will not be able to hold others accountable. Learn that every choice you make in your life, whether influenced or not, was yours to make. You create your reality and livelihood by the choices you make. If you choose to find the lesson you'll see it. If you choose to be angry, anger will consume you. Once you learn you and you alone control your life you will learn that it is all self inflicted. Discipline is foreign to a lot of us. Our parents, some of them, only showed us discipline in a negative light. Some of them often went back on their word, and because you were innocent and a child you could not call them on it. As an adult you must learn you are not your parents nor their life choices. Do what you say you are going to do and communicate if there is a change of plans. Time is the only thing you can't get back or repay. So take others time as serious as you take your own ticking death clock. Learn to spot check yourself on the issues in the moment. You can't grow putting it off every chance you get. Discipline yourself. Learn that you can always grow from a situation. Account for your words, actions, truths, and all things you, be it comfortable or uncomfortable.

Dreams

Do not ever let anyone keep you from your dreams. Those that attempt to do so are selfish and you should cut ties. Dreams exist because of a higher self believing in your greatness and potential. Who are you to keep yourself from your own definition of success? Imagine letting someone keep you from your dreams, then they turn around and leave you in your tracks to go pursue their dreams that do not include you… People are not our possessions. If the growth is not the same cut the line before you both drown. You can't save others without first saving you. Your dreams never die. Your desire to bring them to fruition do tho. Your persistence lacks. You legit should stop half ass'n yourself. Stop half loving yourself. You have to be, you need to be, whole by yourself to complement another human. Date yourself so you will know what your dream date looks like. Be friends with yourself so you can know how to befriend others. You can't be anything to anyone without first being it to and for yourself. Support your own dreams so you are not talking others out of theirs.

Choices

Stop going along with things that make you uncomfortable and things you do not want to do. If you do not voice it, they will never know. If they get offended that is personal and their problem not yours. If they cared about you they would understand boundaries. They would also voice what bothers them. Stop blindly leading people to your love language. Your heart nor feelings are a toy. If they are selling you forever dreams, what better time for them to leave than the present?

Does not matter how long it took you to make a mistake. What matters is what you do after you realize what you have done. Do you settle? Do you hold yourself accountable? Do you vocalize your findings to the other human and cut ties if it is not fixed? Who do you love more, yourself or them? Time will only tell. Life is a great deal of choices. Stop letting others choose for you and start choosing for yourself. Place your happiness at the top of every to do list you make.

Possibilities

If it is possible for one it is in fact possible for all. I do not know where that, "that kind of love do not happen for people like me", mentality come from but drop it back the fuck off. Your desires, your aspirations, your manifestations, your words, your thoughts, (you see the common denominator here or must I keep going?) creates your livelihood, your outcome, your environment, your world. You're only defeated when you accept defeat, MENTALLY! Every battle has a winner and a loser. There's a lesson for both parties which makes them both a winner. Determination and Desire is what separate the two. You can be the boss. You can be rich in wealth, health, and currency. You first have to mentally prepare for it. Gradually work towards it. Throughout it all speak it into existence. Think it into reality. Stop accepting mediocrity knowing you still gone die, might as well soar high. Might as well be happy about it while doing it. Start loving self so you can know what love is and what love is not. When you don't know how to love yourself you'll accept any love language in hopes to blindly get it right. When you're unknowing of self you and accountability are never mentioned in the same sentence. Accountability is foreign to you. You'll blame other people and things for whats happening to you. You give away all your power to them and blame them for using it against you. You can't give stipulations on things after giving them away.

You Be You

Be the person that makes you smile. Be the sunshine after the rain for yourself. Be the courage you need to fight another battle. Be the perfect spouse to yourself. Date yourself. Be the perfect parent for yourself. Discipline yourself. Be the perfect friend for yourself. Hold yourself accountable. Realize you are flawed and so the fuck is everyone and everything else. Be the perfect teacher to yourself. SEEK KNOWLEDGE so you can never say, "I do not know." This is how you teach yourself your own love language. This is how you learn how you desire to be treated.

This is how you stop yourself from settling. If you are everything to and for yourself you will not settle for anything that takes away more value than it adds to your life.

Believe in Yourself

Believe in yourself so much so others negative comments, about your life choices that are not conducive to your livelihood, gets them cutoff after not adhering to the first warning. You can tell yourself all day their words do not bother you but you cannot control your subconscious intake. Memorized behavior and the knowledge of self behavior cannot coexist in one brain. It is a constant battle with self and you lose every time. You have to lose who you are to become who you are supposed to be. The caterpillar does not hold on to his instar each time he sheds his skin. He does not hold onto his caterpillar behavior once he metamorphose into a butterfly. Your faith in yourself should be the strongest faith you own. A lot of shit went down in your life. You lost a lot of shit. You probably gained a bit more but we do not speak of our spiritual gains for some reason. Gained a few friends, loss a few family members to the next realm, had material things, and lost possessions. The only constant in your life is Y O U!! You should celebrate yourself more than you do. You beat, mentally, yourself up every time you do some bad but you do not celebrate your small growth. You should celebrate your small level ups. You should treat yourself more often. You are the only thing you started this life with and you are the only thing that will be there when you end this life. Your belief in yourself teach other people how much they should trust you, and my love, energy does not lie.

Love

Have a love so strong with yourself that every goodbye you have ever had to write in stone still speak your praises and how they know you with a hurt so vivid everyone after you seems to be a seat filler. When you love yourself your soul becomes magnetic to users. If you do not learn to keep them at bay you will end up the hurt one every time. Do not take anything personal nor get hurt by who you wanted them to be. The person hurting you is who they actually are. Learn the magnitude of your power. Discover it!! Tap into it. Never allow another to use it against you. Know your worth. Anything that does not bring you peace is not worthy of your time nor InnerG. Death is inevitable. Why spend any of your time upset, mistreated, miserable, angry, or any emotion of fear that you can control?

Who Got You?

Do not measure your success based on others. You cannot rush greatness. Whether it took thirty days or thirty years is not the topic. All that matters is you achieved it. You did not give up on you. You stayed persistent. You nurtured yourself, but most importantly you believed in Y O U!! Your higher self is always trying to reach you on each level of you. If you feed your subconscious negativity you will manifest negativity. Learn to find the lesson in all things you. Study yourself and know you are human and shit happens. Do not attempt to be anyone but you. Trying to walk in someone else's shadow dims your light and will eventually result in you losing sight of the vulnerable you, mentally, physically, spiritually, and emotionally. You can't be anything to and for anyone else that you are not to yourself. Your journey is yours and yours alone. You wanna do a disservice, by being someone you are not, to the authentic you because why? Your path can't be measured by the steps of others. No two success are the same. What you feed will grow. If you feed the success and health of others over your own what are your expectations? You only get out what you put in. If you desire a certain lifestyle make sure your circle has the same or similar desires otherwise you will never see your desires come to fruition. Your mates desires must mirror or support yours, if not you are in a sinking ship, knowingly.

Do The Choosing

Do not ever let another human decide your fate. You, and only you, should make decisions on your behalf. When you let other people decide you are telling them you do not know your worth. You are telling them you do not love yourself. They will use that against you. They will hurt you with your own words. Do not take it personal tho. They do not love their self either. If they did they would not be using your power against you. Karma knows no timeline. Make sure you are ready for friends, for mates, for any and all relations that require a commitment and you to uphold a half of a ship. You will settle if you let others choose and you will be mad at them instead of yourself when they hurt you.

Nah but For Real

Are you comfortable or are you growing? How do you know? Are you happy? What is the source of that happiness? Are you healthy, mentally? Be sure. No one can live nor die for you, so do not give them the power to make any decisions on your behalf. Love yourself enough to know you can only carry one side of relations with others. You are only responsible for your half of the relations. If the respect not there or the boundaries are crossed to often, check it. They're your drug and you need to rehab yourself before you overdose. Do not let selfish people use you and get away with it. That is stupidity. Yes karma is your life but so is accountability. Check people and yourself when you are tolerating their disrespect. Check them for having the audacity to try you. Check yourself for letting it go on longer than it should have. One time is enough to check it. See people for who they are THE FIRST TIME!! Believe them the first time. Do not fill in the blanks. Do not assume what they meant. Do not make excuses for them. Do not blame yourself, either. GROW THROUGH IT!! If people cared about your existence and valued you, you would not be in the position to choose between your peace and them. A person that loves you unconditionally will never force you to choose. They would reciprocate your behavior and love. How often do you tell yourself, "I love you! I appreciate you!"? Probably not often as you should. Start talking to yourself more often. Look yourself in the eyes in the mirror every morning and speak positively to and about you to set the tone of your day.

Health is Wealth

We live our lives inside of a body and ignore it every time it warns us of illness or disease. When you lack water your body tell you in so many ways. Sudden dry skin, chapped lips, foamy spit, itchy red eyes, pale gums, dry feet and hands, amongst other signs. When there is pain we do not try to figure out why it is there we just rush to make it stop. This does not help, only prolongs the healing and the illness yet does not fix it. Learning your body helps you pinpoint illnesses. What you are eating is either killing you or keeping you alive. If your diet is shit so are you internally. You rarely see obese healthy elders. They often have numerous health issues and live their last days bed ridden. The only thing keeping you alive is your desire to live. If you let your health go, then you are writing your expiration date yourself. People can tell you how bad the food you are ingesting is a million times over, but nothing will change until you desire to change, the knowledge, the healthiest version of you, and the best for yourself. Simple self care goes a long way. A toothache= Brush teeth, floss, and rinse with peroxide. Acne= Drink more water, wash pillow case more often, wash face more, try a clay mask (Indian clay, baking soda, water, an essential oil. Mix and let sit for 30-45min.) Hunger pangs= Drink a full bottle of water. If pangs persist have nutritious snack. If pangs ease drink more water you're dehydrating. Nightly, drink a glass of alkaline water, stretch your limbs, meditate, brush your teeth and repeat in the morning. Life is a bunch of choices, what are you choosing for yourself health wise?

Check Engine Light

Today I had to check myself. I often ask others if they think I was right or wrong about situations I didn't trust my decisions on. Others words don't become true until you give them value. If someones words bother you question your personal beliefs about yourself on the topic. Communicate to understand what they meant to insure your perception isn't off. We don't all think alike. Remember it's not about who's right or wrong but WHAT'S right or wrong. When you have personal attachments to the outcome it's in your human behavior to choose the answers that benefit you regardless if it's right or wrong. Oftentimes we beat ourselves up about our flaws. We should instead, accept them, take accountability for them, and fix them as best you know how. You can't erase them completely because no one is perfect, but you definitely can own, account, and accept them. A few people kept asking me my source, and it bothered me. Made me feel like my knowledge wasn't enough I must have a source and not have experienced it for myself. However, I had to realize I didn't feel like my knowledge was enough. I always question my thoughts and narrative. I credited my words to others so people would believe and go search for themselves. I always looked for sources to seek validation and truth to my words. What I was not understanding was I have grown into the woman I am supposed to be on this level at this frequency. I can no longer be that voiceless little girl, in any aspect. I am a leader. I have to know it and own it, otherwise a peasants word would knock me off my throne every chance they got. I must know for myself who and what I am. I second guess myself a lot. It is a coping mechanism. I am still growing, and I am still learning. I can teach but I will always be a student first. On the spot checks of yourself helps you grow in real time instead of making excuses for your behavior then saying it takes time. Time is of the essence and there is no time like the present.

Mirror, Mirror

It is so easy for us to see others problems and issues while ignoring our own. COPING MECHANISM!! Start turning the mirror on yourself and you will see the part of others in you that you can pinpoint in them. Why is it you can vividly see this flaw? Does it remind you of a part of you that you suppress to impress others? Is it a part of you that you are running from? Are you willing to face your own music or just point out the imperfections of others? You can lie to the world all you want, unless you believe your own lies, you're dying inside. A compulsive liar lives a creative yet miserable life. They are constantly concocting new lies to feed their addiction. They cannot be wrong nor can your situation ever be worst than theirs, unless you start lying too. Speak, walk, talk, live, be content, be accountable, most importantly BE FUCKING HAPPY, in your truth.

Growing Parents

How much do you really love your seeds? Do you take parenting serious? Are you growing daily so you can make sure your child is growing into who they are destined to be? A lot of parents push their beliefs off and onto their children with no research done on the parents part. When you are not growing neither is your child. If you recollect your life and your hobbies and they are the exact same pre-parenthood YOU ARE NOT GROWING!!! Start self reflecting and seeking areas that need change. Change does not happen without action. You are your child's lifeline to the world. A lack of growth is a setup for failure and a slow and steady painful mental death. You can't say you love your child and in the same breath give them a lesser version of yourself than a growing one. Growth is a life-long process. If you are stagnant it is disrespectful to your child in the form of mental abuse. Your child did not ask to be here. Your child do not know growth if you are not teaching them growth. Your child did not ask for stagnant growth. Your choices impact your child's life more than you can imagine. Things that are small to you can last days on your child's mind and become traumatic. Some day your child will hold you accountable for the part you played in who they are becoming. Will your effect be negative or positive? Will you receive praise for your unconditional love? Will you receive recognition for how amazing you were truthfully, or will your child be forced to create an image of you they desire you to be to the world as they know it?

Truth Hurts

When you ignore your flaws, and lie to yourself about yourself, hearing about them from others is painful. This is why it is important to embrace and face your truth, good and bad, while growing through it in real time. You are defensive of yourself against others because truth hurts. You can't defend yourself against your subconscious but you can defend yourself against the world. Truth hurts even if the delivery is from someone you hold near and dear to your heart. Truth hurts even if it comes in the form of help with a good delivery. Fix yourself instead of being easily angered by the words of others. Account for your actions and let them know your intentions were not malicious or to hurt anyone. Account for your flaw and communicate that you are working on said flaw. Hurt people will hurt people, mostly unintentionally. You can't give what you do not possess. Your actions speak far louder than any sentence you can concoct. Be honest with yourself so you can be honest with others.

Sometimes we lie to ourself so much for so long, we begin to believe our own lies while creating false narratives and realities. Treat yourself the way you desire to be treated so you will know exactly how you want others to treat you. You do not want others being dishonest with you. You do not want others intentionally hurting you. You do not want others to disrespect you. You want the people around you to reciprocate your innerG.

I Can't Make You

You can't force anyone to do anything they do not want to do. You can try but if they are not willing to do it, it is not happening. You can, however, find them a replacement. You can't force but you are entitled to replace, be it platonic or intimate. Stop exhausting your energy on people that do not want to change. It is one thing to grow together, it is another to beg someone to be who you desire them to be. How it starts is how it should continue and/or end. Ignoring red flags in the lust phase will become a problem when the lust leave your eyes. Stop trying to force conversations if they do not want to communicate. You do not have to raise a mate to have a mate. Not a soul got you the way Y O U got you. You are not a professional human groomer. It is not your job to teach or heal the other half of relationships you are in. You are only responsible for your half. You are the only one responsible for you. You are the only one that gets to live and die for you. I can't stress to you enough how unhealthy it is to try and carry both halves of a relation. The title ain't shit if it does not bring you more peace than pain. You can't blame others for your hurt feelings when you are the one allowing them to continue to hurt you. Hold yourself accountable. You should know you can't force the lock if the key got different grooves. History taught you that. Try to put a key in a lock with different grooves too many times you will damage both the lock and the damn key simultaneously.

Heal Yourself

Heal yourself before moving on to other relations after being hurt. Do not make your next mate pay for past karmic relations and mishaps. You can't complement anyone if you yourself are not healed and complete. While healing you should spend as much time as you need alone. Do not put off time alone because of things and humans you can live without. Do not underestimate the influence the vibe and energy others have on you. Energy is contagious. You can't heal in the same environment that broke you. Toxicity breeds toxicity. Positivity breeds positivity. During your healing be patient with yourself. When shit gets tough take a break, mentally and physically. This is your first time at this task and on this path. No one has walked this path prior to you, for your life journey is yours and yours alone. Only you can complete your journey regardless of who you choose to bring along for the ride, seasonal or long term. You deserve healthy relations, but you have to be healthy to receive them wholeheartedly. You get what you give. Heal, beloved. Grow, beloved. Love, beloved.

Self Healing Instructions

At some point you must face your childhood trauma and hold your parents accountable so you can in time hold yourself accountable . This is the first step in getting to know and healing self. If you can't communicate with your parents you surely can't communicate with the rest of the world. After you face your parents you must face yourself. Hold yourself accountable for all of your choices. Learn your behavior so you can start distinguishing between your coping mechanisms and your actual personality. After you face yourself, learn your love language. Forget everything you think you know about love and were taught it should be or look like. Love yourself. Love you flaws. Love your growth and your healing. Be patient with yourself. Understand you are not perfect and will make mistakes. After learning your love language, befriend your-self. Date yourself. Love yourself!! Treat yourself. Hang out with yourself. Choose yourself each time you have to choose between you, your peace, space, time, and someone else. You teach people how to treat you by how you treat you and your tolerance of how they treat you.

Relationships
(Or what we know them as)

Having healthy relationships is as important as healthy physical and medical appearance. When you've never seen one anything toxic is acceptable for you. You'll even try to convince those around you that its normal. If you have never witnessed a healthy ship, WHEW!!! Relationships are case to case, however human behavior is universal. A liar as a mate does not think an honest mate exist. A cheater does not think an honest monogamous/polygamous ship exist. A hopeless romantic expect others to also be blinded by love. Now we did not get this way overnight. Your parents, aunts, uncles, elders, neighbors, whomever had a hand in your growth during your impressionable years molded you this way. We learn from what we see. Every toddler mimics their parents behavior and repeat their parents words at some point. It is naturally how we learn, through repetition and seeing. Along the way we develop our own unique learning pattern that is more comfortable for how we intake information. Science claims there is only a number of learning patterns, but truth is exposed by experience. Experience has shown people learning shit in ways unexplained or labeled. The best relation to have is the one you have with yourself. If you do not have a relationship with yourself how could you possibly have one with anyone else? How could you know what it looks, feels, or supposed to be like? People treat others how they treat themselves. Naturally if you put yourself second, you will put others second subconsciously. When you normalize toxic behavior you defend it. You get defensive when someone brings it up. A relationship with self will teach you, we are mirrors. If I call you on something my perception of your behavior is my thoughts when I behaved in that manner. Growth is being able to hold the mirror up and checking yourself. Fixing from within. Yo should not expect others to do things you are not willing to do for them. Reciprocity is everything. It is balance, most importantly. If we learned this early on cheaters would not play the reverse psychology game of accusing the mate of cheating just because their conscious is eating at them. It is their tale tale sign of infidelity.

But Did You Try

Do not knock it til you try it. We will say no to something without thought, try it. The next time someone ask you a question observe yourself and how much thought you give your answer. How do you know you dislike something if you've never tried it? Opportunity is everything. When you are not used to having things you say no because you could not afford it once upon a time, or you had a negative experience too many when saying yes. What are you afraid of when opportunity is free? You can't live a life of peace in fear. Fearing the unknown does not change its existence. Be more diverse. Be more open. Try most things once. What does not kill you will give you memories.

Let's Chat

Communicate with your child more than you talk at them.
HEAR them!!!! You had your chance to grow. You have your
outcome. Do not pawn your ideal human off on your child.
That is selfish. That is wrong as fuck. Your child did not ask to
be here. Account for your choices and grow in real time. You
can't be stagnant on your child's time. You owe it to them to be
the best you at every level of growth with transparency. Be
honest with your child. One day they will learn your lies are
not true and the outcome will not always be in your favor. Do
not teach your child it is ok to choose material possessions
over human relations. You may acquire another job, you may
purchase another or newer car, but you cannot get back time
or replace memories. Your child will not remember the fancy
make and model of the toys you bought, however they will
remember the missed memories and your absence at their
most important moments.

Newsflash

I discovered it is not what others think of you, it is what you think of yourself. We think it often and do not address it aloud with self, or we say it aloud to see if others agree. Perception is everything. Everything is beautiful, a yes, and right from someone's view. Love your natural self so you never wear a facade of self love. Stop devaluing yourself. You are worthy. You are lovable. You are valuable. You are deserving. You are wealthy. You are beautiful. You are GOALS! You have to know all these things and desire the manifestation of them in your reality, first, in order to attain them.

Make It Your Own

Do not let others set your boundaries. Only you know what is best for you. Only you have lived for and with you up until this point. Only you can decide for you. Make it your own; be it jobs, careers, life path, journeys, relationships, friendships, parenting, hobbies, adulting, livelihood, and all things you. You do not have to follow any set of rules. You do not have to wait for anyone's approval. You do not owe anyone an explanation. What works for you could very well not work for the next person. You do not have to like and or agree with others healthy choices, but you must respect them. As long as they are not causing anyone else harm let them live. Stop living in fear, I meant misery, because you care to make others happy. Live for you. Do it only if you want to, not because you "have" to or others want you to do it. Your journey is yours for a reason. It would be a waste to live it on others terms and accord. No two stories are the same, so no two set of rules are the same. Chemicals may be your vice while herbal is mine.

You are Free To Be

We internalize our struggle so much so that it bothers us when others speak on their struggle. We atrocity compare and harbor feelings. If you are harboring hate happiness can't pull in the port. You can't be bitter about it if you are not communicating what it is. Not only to the other human but also to yourself. Speak freely about your pain. You speak about all your good without stuttering. Complaining and communicating, for healing and understanding, is two different things. Do not let someone else dictate to you what you can and can't speak on. Do not let someone else tell you what you should or should not speak on. It is your life and your problems. It is your truth. If people cared how you spoke of them they would treat you as such. Do what you need to do aloud and remember mind over matter. Just believe. You have to have a balance otherwise it is two extremities. When you are good it is all roses and sunshine, but when you are mad it is destructive damaging hurricanes and tornadoes galore. Be kind to yourself. You do not have to prove yourself to anyone. You do not owe anyone. You are not you without you.

LIFE MESSAGES

The truth is if you can find the desire within and stay per-sistent you can change your story to in time change your life.

Who you spend the most time with is who you become. How often are you alone? That is how much of yourself you are. Raise your standards of yourself. Think highly of yourself and speak positive to and about yourself. The world got you on the criticism department so you be gentle in how you discipline Y O U!!

The lack of resources is the problem when you playing the blame game. The lack of resourceful- ness is the problem when you hold yourself ac- countable. The canceling procrastination and ex- cuses is the solution.

Decisions determine your life. They determine your conditions as well, NOT THE OTHER WAY AROUND!! You decide what you focus on. If your focus is on the negative you will never see the positive. You decide if you allow others and the action of others to choose your focus. If you do not take control of your focus someone else will. Focus on your present so you do not miss the moment.

Do not project your thoughts onto others. Ask questions if you feel a certain kind of way but do not assume your thoughts are their truth. Communicate for understanding when doing so.

Contentment is a beautiful thing. We are so caught up in currency we ignore passion. The cost of living so high we can't focus on who and what we are. Instead of changing the system we internalize the struggle and suffer in agreement while thinking average tokens are privilege.

Do not limit yourself. You have infinite potential until you decide your limitations. The thoughts manifest into reality. Defeat happens mentally before it ever becomes physically. Think as a survivor. Think as a winner. Become your truth. Live your best life. You do not have to retaliate, or become the person hurting you, to prove your strength. If you do not feel how they feel you can give them the space to express their frustration. If they are hurtful in their words and actions address it without becoming them. If they are in denial you let them go. They have room to grow and not at the expense of abusing you in any form. It is best to cut ties than to allow the hurt to get to a level of forced ejection.

Stop playing the blame game. You are responsible for how you react. You choose your actions. Just because they did not give the desired reaction does not mean you blame them for your choices. Be genuine in your giving of self.

What is the one thing you love doing so much so you'd do it for free? That's ya passion. That's ya purpose. Do that to change lives. The currency will come just do it your way and be authentic.

If you do not heal you become what broke you.

Compete with the person you are destined to be and stop competing with others. Self growth more valuable than simple bragging rights.

Who will take
care of you if
you do not take
care of you?

Learn from the experience of life. Be nice to yourself. Be upfront with people. Tell them what you desire and need in order for the relation to work for you. Allow them the choice to walk if they can't deliver. Being upfront will save you from long term trauma.

Do not follow their words.
Let their action lead your
decisions.

Read the ingredients of everything you ingest. If you do not know it, google it. Stop eating poison and blaming genetics for your shitty health. You ate your way there.

What are your expectations of life? What is your ideal day? What do you expect of your experience? What is your approval of yourself? Do you really love yourself? Do your actions mirror those words? Are your expectations of yourself high?

Do not dismiss the best parts of you by trying to define yourself to fit society's normal. Live your best life aloud, unapologetically, and without fear of being judged. Those that mind do not matter, and those that matter do not mind.

Make sure you are doing it because you want to. That way regardless of their actions, your reaction is one of contentment because you were only speaking your truth.

If you do not heal you become what broke you.

It is your responsibility to heal yourself. It is not your mates nor any human outside of you. Traumatic experiences aren't who you are. You are not your coping mechanisms. Your personality is waiting for you to drop the facade and admit you have issues. Start healing.

Allow yourself freedom. Do not box your feelings or personality. Do not make yourself feel smaller to make others feel average. Do not mute your voice. Speak your truth. There is a difference in malicious intent and honesty. Vibes do not lie.

There is no statue of limitation on love. There is no limit on how often or how soon you can love. There is no bounds to love. There are no rules in love. Humans complicate love. Humans try to define love and make it definite. Lose everything you've been taught of love and trust again.

Do not hold your past against yourself. Forgive yourself. Account for your actions and grow through and from them. You can't forgive others if you are unforgiving of yourself. Perfection does not exist. We are all flawed and got issues.

Your choices tell a lot about how you feel about yourself. If you do not feel worthy you let others treat you as such. You will even treat others like shit.

Before acting, ask yourself, "How would I feel if someone did what I am about to do, to me?"

Ask your mate, "How does it feel to be loved by me?". Make them feel like they are speaking your positive but you listen for what you are not doing. Listen with the intent to become a better you.

Live without explanation. Stop doing stuff to prove your love, to prove your loyalty, to prove your (wo)manhood. You know who and what you are. You do not owe anyone an explanation. Their expectations of you are their own personal problem. You can't live up to your own expectations and who this world wants you to be too.

Work on yourself before you go telling someone else what they need to work on Mr./Miss Mirror! The blame game gets you nowhere in or with love. Be vulnerable and create a space of transparency on your half of the relations. Be what you want so when someone you desire is not, you can walk because your solitude is better than any settlement.

You are not obligated to settle for less than you are willing to give. Your choices are yours and yours alone. If you are healing you should not be dating; you will hurt others and be hurt, sometimes beyond repair. You can't play the blame game when it comes to love. Problems exist where communication does not. You have to communicate your anger, not show it. You do not get mad because someone else is mad, just how much of you are you letting someone else control?

You can't force it. You can be a mansion on the oceanside fully furnished, four car garage, two motorcycles, and the dog. If they are not ready for you they will miss the intricate architectural detailed work of the foyer, they will miss the tempered crystal floor salt water pool, they will miss the little detailed designs and the imported family made fabric. If their focus not on you then you focus on you and fine tune your mate requirements and the prerequisites of being with you.

Your secret weapon is Y O U! No one could be you. No one could think your unique thoughts. They can bite it, but no one can ever do you the way you boss up and do you. No one can walk in your shoes and survive the way you did. Things you have been through would have stopped the growth of others because growth takes strength and is far from conventional. Do not mute your voice, be it your comfortable or uncomfortable truth. Telling people your dream does not change the outcome of it becoming your reality. Your persistence, drive, ambition, determination, motivation, desire, and need, or lack thereof changes your outcome. If you did not succeed you gave up just an unexpected no too soon. Do not live your life expecting anything from anyone but yourself otherwise you are asking for disappointment if your expectations are not met. Life is short. If you are ever afforded the opportunity to bring yourself healthy pleasure, DO IT without hesitation.

Just do it! If the desire is there JUST FUCKING DO IT!! No you do not know what will happen, but if you never take the first step the top of the staircase will forever remain a mystery. You are the resource. Just believe in yourself and start. You will get there. I have faith in you, and I need you to have faith in you too. You deserve a happy life created by you and centered on you. If you not the center of your world you are a pawn in someone else world.

Fast once a week from your daily routine. Take a day just of you. No outsiders. No food. No work. Just relax and be with yourself. It helps you to stop over exhausting yourself mentally, physically, and emotionally. You need you more than anything else.

People that do not get to know self will have an immeasurable void they are attempting to fill. They will go from mate to mate, have child after child, befriend friend after friend, have drunk night after drunk night. Anything but their reality will do. You can't fill the void of self without learning and knowing self first.

Allow others to do what makes them happy. If it does not align with your choosing and livelihood, you should skip that relation. Do not try to change others or "fix" them to your liking. You are dismissing the best parts of them.

Telling someone one thing while simultaneously doing the opposite is mental and emotional abuse. Very unhealthy and should be addressed. If not changed it should be left. You can't heal still being hurt.

Who is they? They said. They will think. Most importantly why do you care about they? They do not take care of you physically nor mentally, thats your job. They DO NOT KNOW YOU! If they knew you they would have no room to judge you. Next time you are enjoying life and someone interrupts your fun mentioning outsiders in the manner of what "they" would think of your behavior ask them, "When was the last time your thoughts and actions were that of your own and not to impress they?". "They" do not care about you or my well being. They just need a scapegoat and new gossip material to help them avoid their own reality. Your life is "they" entertainment. Your life interest "they" and their boring life choices.

\

People treat you how they feel about you. Deafen your ears to their noise of words and open your eyes to their actions. You will learn a lot about how the person feel about you and themselves as well.

If you want a different outcome do different shit. Do not allow your past to use you as a revolving door. Account for the choices you are making. If it was meant to be it would have been. Find the lesson and leave the human with less damage than you found them.

Your intentions may be great, but your execution could be the issue. Be understanding. Be an ear. Be the shoulder you needed when you were going through that last time. Listen to the other person the way you wish someone would listen to you. Do not make excuses. Be accountable. You have to understand you are the bad person in some stories, and accept it. You are not perfect. You will make errors along the way. You are not perfect. The mistake is not the problem, what you do after you find out you are the villain in said story is what really counts.

If you care and want to know COMMUNICATE IT! Do not let the actions of others dictate your feelings towards them or the situation otherwise your feelings were conditional. If someone you love stops communicating with you, ASK THEM WHY! Do not ask around them. Do not assume you know why. Do not try to get even or be malicious as an excuse of care. You can care positively and still get your point across.

Be good at everything
you do, and you do not
have to do much.

Stop settling and expecting others to abide by your stipulations you created because of your choices. It is no one's fault but your own that you settled. You chose to settle. No one forced your hand. You can't blame the other person or hold your settling over their head. You know your worth, or do you? You do the walking when it no longer grows or becomes you. You can't be mad at anyone but yourself for what you chose.

It is not the best you could do, it is the best you decided to do. Raise your standards of yourself. Stop shortchanging yourself with mediocrity for the sake of comfortability. Expect more of yourself.

State your boundaries and relationship terms upfront when entering new relations. Give them the opportunity to choose to accept or decline these terms. Respect their honesty. If they can't oblige then it is up to you whether you settle for allowing them to treat you how they want to and not how you desire to be treated.

Be honest about your feelings. The other person does not have to reciprocate the feelings but be honest with them and yourself anyways. Do not suppress your feelings because they are not acting in the desired manner you thought out in your head. You do not have to care what others think when it comes to you. Express yourself freely as long as you are not imposing on someone else or their health.

How often are you checking your growth?
How often you ask your friends, "How am
I as a friend?". How often you ask yourself,
"do you really love me?". How often are you
accounting for your lacking? Start checking
yourself. It is not always other people.
Make sure your communication is under-
standable, not because you think so but because you've allowed the person you are
communicating with the vulnerable space of
truths; be it comforting or uncomfortable.

Trust and forgiveness is mostly done from memory. Start seeing each person with a new lens, hell change the camera. Just because the last person did not accept you for you doesn't mean the next person will do or be the same.

Your happiness and your purpose have strong ties. Lose the money over everything mentality. Pick up the memories over currency, family over come ups, and friends before dollar amounts mentalities.

If your new relation is the same or resembles your last relation you are not growing. You are repeating lessons. You are stagnant in conventional growth. You are fighting with your higher self instead of letting them lead the way. Obviously greater is out there for you if you just get out of your own way.

Heal that hurt in your heart so you can hear your own voice. When you harbor hurt you are dealing with the voice of your inner child, the voice of who others want you to be, the voice of who you want to be, and the voice of who you need to be. Stop people pleasing and start self pleasing. You can please others simply by pleasing yourself.

Be you authentically and unapologetically. You never know who you
are inspiring and who is counting on
you. Most importantly make
sure....you are watching and inspiring yourself and you are someone
YOU can count on.

Focus on your positives. Focus on your goals. Focus on your capabilities. You become what you focus on and think. Yes the negative is there but it is only negative when you give it that energy. Approach negativity with understanding and lesson to be learned thoughts. If you keep seeing negative you need to self check.

If you can look at a relationship you are in and accept your other half treating you any kind of way or not reciprocating then believe you me beloved, YOU ARE SETTLING!! You are what you accept. If you accept that mediocrity you become it, it consumes you, and you waddle in it.

Build the person you want to be so you can have the life you desire to have. It will not fall in your lap. You can't be mediocre and expect greatness to blossom in your life. You have to go above and beyond if you want extraordinary and extravagance.

Change your habits. Most of them are coping mecha-nisms anyway if we being honest.

The way you begin each day is the way you will live each day. The first conversation of each day should be had with yourself. Speak positive to and about you, daily. Stand in front the mirror and appreciate yourself, daily with gratitude.

Be disciplined in your growth. Be consistent in your reciprocity. Be persistent in your accountability.

Work smart not hard. If you missing meals to do it, you may want to reevaluate why you are doing it in the first place. Your health is your wealth. You would not be able to do it without you.

Do not confuse busy with pro-gression. A relaxed mind is a free mind. A free mind is a creative mind.

When you start feeling doubtful, re-place those those with you thinking of your goals. When you feel the need to gossip, instead discuss your goals and how you can achieve them. When you feel the urge to lie, remember to stop yourself and correct it on the spot. When overthink, replace it with posi-tive outcomes and thoughts of you achieving your goals.

Failure does not exist, only lessons learned. Be disciplined. Do not give up on you. Stay the course despite the obstacles, seen and unforeseen. Do not stop until your dreams are your reality.

Lower your tolerance for bull shit. Be disciplined in your on doings so you choose better people.

People will project their fears onto you telling you things can't be done, but DO NOT LISTEN!!! These people will often be people you respect and look up to, but still do not listen. ABORT MISSION LISTENING!!! They lack the courage, confidence, ambition, desire, dream, vision, and morals of you. They project their imaginations onto you without seeing your vision from your sight of view and your predicted outcome.

Do something you do not think you are capable of doing. Start small so habit forms over time. Believe you can. Envision yourself doing it. Be persistent and you will achieve it.

Nothing worth having was ever given instantly. Focus on the steps you have taken and the steps you can take. Do not focus on what you think you are lacking. You will attain all you need if you stay the course and never give up on you. What you feed will grow and all things take time, beloved.

There is no easy way out.
Try a bunch of ways until
you find one to make it
your own.

Your right now is not your forever so live in your moments more than you wish them over. You can never get that moment back and you deserve to experience all your moments in depth. Be present, not just there.

Success is for the persistent.

Ensure it is not just achievable but also sustainable, too. Longevity over instant gratification.

Do not be afraid to ask for help. The goal is to succeed. Your priority is reaching your goal. A little help goes a long way.

Do not give up your values,
morals, self respect, decency,
and self love for temporary
"needs".

Make new memories. You were innocent when you learned most of your habits and answers to life. You have the power to change the way you move and think. You are no longer controlled. You are free to do as you want as often and as long as you please.

Your brain is a tool. It is yours to use or someone else's to control. You are doing yourself a disservice if you do not train your brain to work for you and no one else.

Sometimes you have to lose it all in order to gain your true desires. Be prepared and like water. No matter what happens to you be you.

Sacrifice is what you are willing to give up. Comfort is what you have to lose. Growth is what you will attain.

Do not be what people want you to be. That is not what life is about. Life is about being you and attracting someone that loves every part of you.

Try it. Do that one thing that scares you. Rid yourself of everything weighing you down before the weight of it, toxicity, breaks you and forces the growth. You can't really grow when it is forced. Adjust your crown and move accordingly.

Stop doing what you feel obligated to do, and start doing all the things you desire to do. Only your belief in that obligation makes it an obligation.

If you ever find yourself in competition I hope it is with the person you were yesterday or even the person you were a few hours back. Anything other than that just won't do. When you compete you focus on the opposition. If your opposition is someone else you are focused on them and not your mission at hand. If you are focused on someone else you are neglecting your growth. You are concerned about how much better you are or can be than some temporary human.

Delay is not denial. Trust your-self and your process. Stay per-sistent yet fluent. Be like water, yourself in every form. Know you need room to grow but be disciplined in that growth. Pro-crastination is not extra time, it is quite the opposite. Live your best life but sure it is not a lie and it is of your choosing.

Beating your child forces them to equate discipline with pain so they run from it in fear. Discipline is not painful. The lack of discipline is. When you are disciplined you know you are going to make mistakes so you give yourself room to do so while simultaneously accounting for your behavior. When you equate pain with discipline you tend to lie in fear the pain is going to be worst than the last time.

I wish we were all raised on love and not fear. So many of us never shake that fear. When fear festers it spread like wildfires, turns into doubts and toxicity, and is very contagious. When you live in fear you are afraid sometimes for no particular reason with no clue as to why. Fear breeds negativity. Love breeds positivity. (Fine tune your definition of love. Sometimes it comes in a facade so be mindful of what you call love.)

The healthier you are the more your body communicates with you and you can under-stand the signs. mental-ly, physically, spiritual-ly, and emotionally.

If you feel you can't help yourself it is ok to seek outside help. It is ok to be vulnerable. Acting tough hurts no one but you. It is ok to walk away. Staying and being miserable hurts no one but you. Self control and self love and self knowledge is the ultimate level up.

If you stop caring what other people think of you, your communication will strengthen tremendously.

If you stab someone what happens immediately after is very vital to their demise or survival. If you take the knife out without plugging the hole, they will bleed out and die in a matter of minutes. If you leave the knife in without keeping them calm and reassured, still they will drown in their own blood and die. It is the same with hurting someone close to you. Your words. Your actions. Your doings all effect them. In other words, stop intentionally hurting people unless your intent is to kill them, spiritually. You do not deserve human relations if that is ever your intent, FYI.

Take care of yourself before you offer your assistance to better someone else. You need all of you more than they desire a piece of you.

Replace your negative thoughts with positive thoughts, as soon as they show up and you feel yourself thinking them.

See yourself there before you reach your goals. Celebrate the small steps to make the big achievement that much more worth getting to. See your success and build on it. You can't stop the obstacles but you can pay em no mind. Only focus on the lesson, not the issue or human giving it.

Do not fake it for other people. If that shit ain't for you let it go, and stay far away from it. You don't owe people shit.

Be sure to never walk in anyone else's shadow, for you may need your own to guide you back to yourself.

Be you unapologetically and fiercely.....just a friendly re-minder.

ABOUT THE AUTHOR

I am an African American on paper. A tomboy from Audra's uterus by way of Montgomery, Alabama. I am proof you can do anything you want to do while being you unapologetically. I have always been me (might have been an altered version on some levels). A permanent vacationer. A healer. A nurturer. A teacher. A solutionist. A leader. I am a nerd in my own light. A weirdo to some. A researcher. I am a world traveler and all things Kris. I hope this book helped you and or gave you clarity you did not have before opening it.